The Giving Heart

MORMON GIRLS

SOPHIE, A KIRTLAND GIRL

Mormon Girls

SOPHIE, A KIRTLAND GIRL

BOOK TWO

The Giving Heart

SUSAN EVANS MCCLOUD
Artwork by Jessica Mormann Chopelas

BOOKCRAFT
Salt Lake City, Utah

Library of Congress Catalog Card Number: 95-77042
ISBN 0-88494-994-X

Second Printing, 1995

Printed in the United States of America

For Mairi,
my last Mormon girl—
the wonder and joy of her spirit
in my life increases and grows sweeter
each day

The author and the artist acknowledge with pleasure and gratitude the invaluable assistance of Dr. Carma DeJong Anderson, who gave countless hours of counsel and instruction, and made available her wide library of resources and the even more impressive resource of her own knowledge and love of historical costume and design to assist this work.

CONTENTS

Chapter One

MUST YOU GO, FATHER?

"Catch that little striped one! He's heading straight for the river!"

Sophie and Ellen laughed as Oscar pounced on the kitten and the two tumbled roly-poly along the green bank. Sophie was happy. The spring day was as warm as mid-summer. She could smell the sweet new grasses, the lilies of the valley, and the delicate white violets which brightened the muddy, color-less marshes that bordered the water.

Sophie tickled Lucy Anne's feet where she lay stretched out on a quilt in the sun. The baby giggled and Sophie bent down to kiss her cheek, more soft, more sweet-smelling than all the spring flowers together.

"You love her very much, don't you?" Ellen smiled as she asked the question. "You don't ever seem to mind watching her, dressing her—even changing her soiled nappies." Ellen screwed her face into an expression of such distaste that Sophie had to laugh out loud. "I dislike taking care of my brothers," Ellen persisted, glancing to where the two little boys were playing.

"It's different with me and Lucy Anne," Sophie said quietly. How could she explain? "First of all, she's a girl—not a boy! And we could so easily have lost her . . ." She paused, the pain of those dark days gathering again in her throat. "Mother, too." Her voice was almost a whisper. "We nearly lost her. But instead—" She looked up and smiled through moist eyes. "But instead, just see what we got!"

It was more than that, though. It was everything that had happened: giving away her precious cat, Aurora, learning how much Mother loved her—so many things she could not find words to express.

"Yes, she certainly is a beauty," Ellen cooed.

Sophie was glad to have Ellen for a friend—Ellen who had come as a stranger to their door last autumn with her basket of kittens and been turned

reluctantly away, only to have Mother go back for the runt of the litter, whom Sophie dubbed only "kitty," later calling her "Willow" so that the poor gray striped kitten would have a proper name. During the cold winter months, attending Mr. Miller's school together, Sophie and Ellen had become best of friends. Now here they sat, eating a picnic lunch by the river, with a new batch of kittens, just as Ellen had promised, and the long spring and summer before them.

"My father nearly agreed to join the men who are going to march to Missouri. I was so afraid that he would." Ellen sighed as she spoke the words.

"What men, what do you mean?" Sophie asked drowsily. She had stretched out on the blanket beside Lucy Anne and closed her eyes. And the sun warmed her face until she felt like an early apricot being brushed into a soft blush by the strokes of the sun.

"You never know anything, Sophie. Honestly!" Ellen scolded. But her voice was gentle and indulgent. After all, she was a year older than Sophie. And, after all, she loved knowing what Sophie didn't know, and being able to tell.

"They're calling it Zion's Camp. Brother Joseph has asked for five hundred volunteers to go out to Missouri with him. That's nearly a thousand miles away, Sophie! He means to save the Saints there from their enemies, though Father says he doesn't know how we could possibly manage that." Ellen sighed again and gave in to the warmth beating down on her hair. "Let's rest by the baby just a few minutes before calling those bothersome boys."

So they did, until their own hunger aroused them. Then, after a lunch of bread and cheese, dried apples, and pound cake that Ellen's mother had baked fresh that morning, they had foot-races across the long meadow and clambered up the rising bank— at the small boys' insistence— to search out the sparrows' nests and the gray river frogs that would jump up so suddenly and startlingly from the mud at their feet.

Sophie was tired when she reached home and only too happy to wash up and help Mother prepare dinner. Her head nodded over her bowl of chicken soup until Father said gently, "I'll help Mother clean up tonight, my little nut-brown maiden. All that fresh air and sunshine has worn you right out."

Mother smiled at her. "Yes, you may go to bed early with Oscar, dear, if you'd like."

Sophie *was* tired. As she got into her nightgown

and said her prayers her drowsy mind was still warm with the pleasures of the day. But just as she started to climb under the covers she heard her father's voice, from the kitchen—she thought she caught a word that sent a chill through her body and made her throat feel tight. She sat up straight in her bed and held very still. Would he say it again?

"Missouri is so far away, Davey. So much might happen to you." Mother's voice was urgent, though calm.

Father's reply was firm and laced with a happy confidence which sounded almost like laughter. "Under the Prophet's care, Martha, and with the Lord to guide us?"

So it was true! Her father wanted to go on the dangerous trek to Missouri. Oh, what should they do?

Sophie slipped back down to her knees and prayed with all her might that Heavenly Father would make her father come to his senses, and let him stay home. When she climbed into bed she could still hear the rise and fall of her parents' voices from the other end of the cabin. She closed her eyes and tried to cuddle into the warm nest Oscar's sleeping body had made. She tried to ignore the little knot of fear that was growing inside her.

❧

The following morning at the breakfast table Sophie was so quiet that Father asked, "Are you ill, sweetheart?"

When Sophie looked up into the ebony depths of his eyes gazing so kindly upon her, she couldn't help herself. "Oh, Father!" she cried. "Ellen told me about the march to Missouri and that her father won't go. I'm so afraid! I heard you talking to Mother—you won't go, either, will you—you won't leave us—"

Father drew Sophie close to him. "Hush now, daughter," he soothed her. "You are a big enough girl and a wise enough girl to try to understand."

I don't want to understand! Sophie's heart protested. But, once again, she met Father's warm, patient gaze.

"First of all, Sophie, it is the Lord asking us, through his prophet, to go aid our brethren." He put his hand under her chin and lifted her head just a little. "Since I first heard of this religion and believed it to be true I have made it my practice to do whatever the Lord may ask of me—"

"But, Father, I prayed!" Sophie nearly choked on the words as they tumbled out of her. "I prayed that he would let you stay with us."

7

"Sophie, Sophie." Father's voice was still tender, but it had grown somewhat stern. "You did not think before you prayed. Sometimes in our ignorance we ask for things which are not really for our best good—"

"It isn't good for you to stay with us?" Sophie did not understand.

Father tried again. "There are little girls in Missouri, I am sure, whose homes were burned and destroyed by cruel men who then drove their helpless families out into the cold. These little girls, huddling along the snowy banks of the Missouri River, are hungry and frightened, Sophie. They have been praying that Heavenly Father would help them."

Sophie nodded. Tears stung her eyes as she thought of Oscar and little Lucy Anne with nowhere to go and no warm roof to shelter them. The small, simple cabin she stood in seemed suddenly quite dear. She could not imagine being driven from her home!

"Yes, it must be terrible," Father agreed, watching her face.

"But why must *you* be their help?" Sophie persisted, though she felt ashamed of the words.

"Heavenly Father works through us, darling; that is his way. If we bless others, he will bless us. Will you remember that?"

Sophie nodded again, though there was a lump in her throat.

"And try very hard, my nut-brown maiden, to pray for the right things. Pray for faith and goodness and gratitude. God will take care of the rest."

Father's words sounded true. Although she did not thoroughly understand them, they made her feel warm inside—warm and loved. It was another beautiful day. With the sun and the birds and the greening earth to cheer her, Sophie forgot everything but her own pleasure and happiness in the beauties around her that sang such joy to her heart.

Chapter Two

FAREWELL

Sophie had never seen so many people come to meeting before! Wagons clogged the narrow roads and the unplowed fields that bordered the temple site—wagons loaded with children like herself and Oscar. And babies—she had never seen so many beautiful, gurgling, rosy-cheeked babies!

"It's because Brother Joseph is speaking today," Ellen informed her, a bit smugly. "And because he's going to talk about redeeming Zion."

"You mean Missouri?" Sophie asked.

Ellen nodded importantly. "It's going to be very dangerous. And who here has time or money for such an enterprise? As my mother said, we can scarcely take care of ourselves! It is enough that they ask for clothing and bedding for the aid of the Missouri Saints. But to ask for our menfolk as well!"

Sophie could see the Prophet walking from one wagon to another, bending to shake hands with each child, speaking to them gently. She could feel the tenderness of his spirit from here. Now he was lifting a bright-eyed baby up in his arms, and the baby was laughing. How Lucy Anne would enjoy that! But she had gone with Mother and Oscar to find a good place to sit. Father was off somewhere talking with a group of the brethren. But Mother had said Sophie might walk alone with Ellen; that is, if she stayed close.

"Oh dear, my father is calling me. I'd better run now!" Ellen gave Sophie's hand a warm squeeze before she ducked off through the wagons and disappeared into the crowd. *Now, where was it Mother had said she would be sitting?* Sophie fidgeted a little, worried suddenly that she would get lost, which was a terribly undignified thing for a big girl of eight to do! Eight *was* older—eight was very different from seven. Why, hadn't Father baptized her in the river only two months before?

"Now you are truly a Latter-day Saint," he had said, with tears in his black eyes. "You have your own testimony and your own right to call upon the Holy Ghost to guide you."

It had been a solemn and beautiful moment, despite the fact that she had been shivering terribly—even beneath the blanket Mother had wrapped around her wet body. How bright and clean she had felt! How anxious to be good and to make her father proud of her!

Was she walking around in circles? Sophie was so busy trying to find her directions that she did not notice the approach of the tall man. He stood and watched her for a moment before saying, in a voice that thrilled through her, "May I be of some assistance, young sister?"

Sophie looked up into the bluest eyes she had ever seen—blue and deep, and as filled with love as Father's. She did not feel afraid or embarrassed. She found herself telling the Prophet her name and whose daughter she was. And then, suddenly, she told him all the other things she had been holding inside.

Joseph Smith listened, his gaze growing more tender as Sophie poured out her heart. "I'm sorry I am not brave and that I wish my father to stay home with us," she finished, with a long, trembling sigh.

"Ah, but you are honest, Sophie," the tall, fair-haired man replied, "and perhaps more brave than you know."

He stooped down until his face was level with

hers. "Do not fear, little one. As your father promised you, the Lord will take care of his own." He placed his hands on her shoulders. His firm touch sent a warmth through her entire body. "You have so much love to give, Sophie. Don't be stingy with it. Your father isn't."

The Prophet's eyes were dancing now, bright with some kind of happiness Sophie did not understand. But she *felt it,* and she liked the feeling.

"Let love, not fear, dictate your actions—and see what wonderful things happen, my child."

He raised himself to his full height, but as he did so he reached out for her hand. "I can see over the heads of most of the others," he smiled, "and I know just where your mother and the children are."

She let him lead her. The crowds parted at his coming, and eyes lingered on him with warmth and pride. He was Joseph, the Prophet, and they believed him to be what he claimed to be—the mouthpiece of God, the instrument to restore God's truths to the earth and teach people what they needed to know so that they might grow to be like their Heavenly Father and return to live with Him again.

When they reached the bench where Mother was seated, Sophie let go of the big hand with reluctance. President Smith touched his hat to

Mother and talked kindly with her for a few moments. But as he turned to leave he spoke over his shoulder to Sophie. "Remember what I told you," he said. The words rang with a warmth and assurance that tingled through her whole being. There were tears in her eyes as she turned toward Mother and reached for the baby, whose arms were held out to her.

Everything was packed and in readiness. Mother had laundered and mended Father's clothes and tucked food into his saddlebags, simple fare that would keep well on a journey: cheese wrapped in cloth, loaves of fresh bread, bags of dried fruit and dried meat. It was too early in the season to have much produce from  the gardens or to hope for fresh, ripened fruit. Father had polished his tall boots and his leather saddle. The fine, heady smell clung in Sophie's nostrils. She kissed the brown stains on Father's long fingers and he caught her eye and winked.

The last thing he did was to pull Mother's rocker out from its corner by the hearth, seat each one of them in turn, and give them a father's parting blessing. This was his priesthood right. What he pronounced in righteousness, listening to the promptings of the Spirit, God would fulfill. Sophie liked the feeling of his big warm hands on her head. She liked the sound of his words. He blessed them with peace and protection. He blessed Mother with the skills she would need to carry on in his absence, and with the strength and confidence she longed for. He blessed Oscar that he might be obedient and helpful. When he placed his hands on Sophie he blessed her with patience and wisdom beyond her years, and a calming of the fears that always ate at her. Sophie was grateful for that.

She walked out into the narrow, dusty road where Father's horse stood waiting. If she must let him go, she would hold on to the sight of him just as long as she could.

He swung his long leg over the saddle and patted the horse's neck. "The brethren will be waiting."

He looked down at Sophie, thoughtful for a moment. "Bless you, my nut-brown maiden," he said, very softly. "You know, I could not do what I am doing without you and Mother. I could not do it alone. Remember, Sophie, you are a part of everything I shall do while I am away. And I am a part of all you do here—in the sweet little home I love."

His voice sounded funny, as though he were choking on something and could not get out the words. Sophie's own throat burned with the tears she was trying to hold back as she kissed her hand and waved to him—waved until her arm ached, until horse and rider disappeared round the bend.

Chapter Three

THE MEAN OLD MAN

&

"The work will always be here. There will always be more work than we can manage to finish." Mother spoke the words with a smile. "So if you get Oscar out of my hair and spare me a few hours by taking care of the baby, why, you will be helping me, Sophie, even while you and Ellen are having fun."

Sophie kissed Mother's soft white cheek. "I'll be careful, I promise."

She skipped out into the yard where Ellen and her brothers were waiting. Ellen had brought along the wagon her father had made for the children. It had tall, slatted wood sides and was well cushioned with blankets. They settled Lucy Anne inside, along with the hampers of food and two fluffy kittens Ellen had managed to wile away from their mother.

As soon as Ellen gave the signal, the three boys scampered ahead, whistling and hallooing.

"Little boys have so much energy," Sophie sighed, as she tugged at the heavy wagon.

"Let's try to catch up to them!" Ellen cried suddenly. "If we both pull we can get this old contraption fairly flying and give them a run for their money, Sophie. Come on!"

It was amazing. The strength of two seemed to far more than double the strength of one. They *were* fairly flying as they rounded the bend of the road, enveloped in rolls of choking dust clouds churned up from the wagon's wheels.

They did not see the pigs and the old, bent man who was herding them until it was too late. Sophie heard a terrible squeal and then the air seemed churned with the shrill, piercing screams of the pigs' complaining. Ellen put her hands to

her ears. But Sophie stood frozen, watching the pink and black backs of the stout, unhappy animals as they scattered around her feet.

"Look what the deuce you've done now—you fool girls!" The old man thrust his scowling, whiskery face close to Sophie's and shook his stick. "I ought to give you both a good beating."

"It was an accident, sir. Really. We're terribly sorry." Ellen's voice shook as she said the words, but at least she was able to speak.

"First those young rascals come shouting like banshees—now you two nincompoops! Get out of my way." He hit at Sophie's leg with his long walking stick and her skin smarted, even through the folds of her light summer dress.

"Let us help you. We can—," Ellen began. But he waved away her offer before she could fairly get the words spoken.

"I want no part of you. You'd do more harm than good, I'll warrant."

The words were a growl, and his face had grown blacker and angrier the longer he thought about the injustice he had suffered—even though most of his pigs, tottering slowly and grunting as they came, were finding their way back to him.

"You're strangers in these parts. Mormonites, I don't doubt. Well, you'd be wise to stay out of

my way. If I lay my hands on those young roustabouts that ran off laughing at their mischief, I'll take a good inch off their hides."

The man was awful. His sunken cheeks were spotted with age marks and a growth of gray, dirty whiskers. His thin, sparse hair looked like wisps and clumps of old whiskers, and whiskers grew out of his ears. And his eyes were as little and mean as the eyes of the pigs that he drove.

"Don't let me catch sight of you hereabouts again," he growled, his head lowered for attack like an old, stubborn bull. "You understand? It won't go well for you, I can promise, if I catch you on my road again."

He shuffled past them, giving the side of the wagon a sharp rap with his stick as he passed. Lucy Anne started to cry. One of the kittens jumped out through the slats and disappeared into the bushes.

"Oh dear!" Sophie cried.

"The wicked old thing," Ellen muttered. "How dare he strike us! We meant him no harm."

She bent down and lifted the tongue of the wagon, holding the red handle tight in her hand. "Wait until my father hears about this!"

Sophie clutched at her arm. "Oh, please, Ellen! Don't!"

"And why not?" Now that the old man and his pigs were well past them, Ellen's anger was quickly crowding out the fear she had felt.

"If my mother hears of what happened, she'll never let us come here again."

"Well, that's silly!" Ellen gave the wagon a tug and moved forward at a brisk walk.

"It may be silly, but I know my mother," Sophie pleaded. "Especially with Father gone. She's ever so much more careful—"

"And she's overly cautious to start with."

"She can't help that! She doesn't mean to be—" Sophie was feeling altogether miserable. Would it be deceiving her mother simply to not tell her what had happened? Already Sophie longed for the comfort that baring her fears to her mother would bring. But how could she live without these cool afternoons by the river? The sweet berries were ripening and the wildflowers starred the meadows. How dull the days would be if she were forbidden to come here!

"All right," Ellen agreed, after some thought of her own. "I think your course is the wisest, Sophie—at least for now. We'll keep a lookout for the old grouch, and if we see him again . . ."

Sophie shuddered at the thought.

"Well, we'll cross that bridge when we come to it," Ellen concluded in her usual decisive way.

They had forgotten all about catching up to the boys. Instead they pulled the heavy wagon down to the shady elm that stretched its long arms out over the river. Here they played with their dolls and the sleepy kittens while the boys played their noisy games at a distance. It was very pleasant, but Sophie didn't feel quite right. When the boys tumbled down the hill, ravenous with hunger, and Ellen in-structed them in her best motherly, no-nonsense tone, Sophie felt more uncomfortable still.

"You were naughty and thoughtless to that old man," Ellen scolded, and the boys made no move to defend themselves. "But we'll let it pass this time—that is, if you say nothing to our parents of the matter, and if you promise to look out for strangers from now on, at least while we're on the road."

The boys were happy to comply and soon forgot the whole incident. Trailing home slowly, with the shadows lengthening, Sophie knew Oscar was too tired to remember much of anything. Once they were back inside the dim, cool

cabin with Mother, there was so much to be done that Sophie had little time herself to worry about her adventure. After she tucked Lucy Anne snugly into her cradle, there were still the pans to be scoured and the rest of the new peas to shell.

June's late, gentle darkness had settled at last and silenced the hubbub of day when Sophie climbed into her bed. She thought about Father and wondered what he was doing far away in Missouri. But her last thought was of the old man, whose sour face bristled and scowled uncomfortably at the back of her mind.

A letter from Father! This was too good to be true. Sophie touched the thin paper lovingly. Mother settled into her rocker, with Lucy Anne on her lap. Sophie and Oscar sat on the rug at her feet.

The letter was postmarked Indiana, and it looked as though it had traveled a long way before it found its way home. " 'My dearest family,' " Mother began reading. " 'I have just come from meeting, and now sit in the quiet of my tent to pen a few lines. I am well; all is well in the camp. Brother Joseph has organized us into

companies of twelve with a captain over each—and I have been elected captain of a very fine group of men.' "

Mother looked up from the paper and smiled at Sophie. Her eyes were so tender that it hurt Sophie to look into them. "The men in that company are lucky," Sophie said, and Mother nodded.

" 'Each company has two cooks, two firemen, two tent men, two watermen, two wagoners and horsemen, and a runner. Also a commissary. Can you think of anything else we might need?' "

Oscar giggled. "They need a boy to keep their boots polished. I told Father so when he left. I could have gone along, I could have kept all their boots clean and shiny."

"You and half a dozen others!" Sophie prodded. But she leaned over and gave his hand a warm squeeze.

" 'We cook our own food, which is generally good, though sometimes scanty. When we have flour enough, we even bake our own bread. We have one young fellow, Martha, who makes johnnycake that would positively melt in your mouth.' "

Mother's cheeks flushed and she clucked under her tongue at Father's words. He was teasing her, for he knew very well that she could not abide johnnycake. Sophie could see the sparkle in

Father's dark eyes as he thought about Mother and wrote those words. She sighed. This was nice. This was like having Father right here in the room beside them.

" 'The sound of a trumpet calls us to our rest each night. But, before laying our heads on our pillows, all the men in their tents kneel before the Lord. We thank him for our blessings and place our service—our very lives—in his hands. As I hope you are doing, my precious ones. I pray for you every morning, every night—every waking moment. May the Lord bless and keep you, and may you remember how much I love you.' "

There were tears in Mother's eyes as she laid down the letter and gathered the children to her. Sophie, nestled against her mother's warm fragrance, thought: *I will remember what Father told me. I will try to be as good and as brave as he is.*

Chapter
Four

RETURNING GOOD
FOR EVIL

The July days were scorching. The beans and tomato vines wilted; the cornstalks drooped. The animals were listless, moving about as little as possible. And Lucy Anne was fussy with a prickly-heat rash. If Mother fired up the oven to cook, the house was too stifling to bear. So many of their meals consisted of salad greens and ripe fruit. Mother would rise early, before the hot, breathless hours of the day, to bottle jam and preserves against the long winter months. The days passed slowly, and they were not as pleasant as the happy June days had been.

Then one day Sophie woke up to a dim gray stillness—so welcome after the glaring light of the hot sun. A storm was coming at last. Moisture for the crops. Moisture to cool the air, fill the water barrels, and wash off the dust. Sophie watched all morning as the clouds built and darkened. She felt a little cross and impatient. Would the rain never come?

Lucy Anne was cross, too. Her itchy rash persisted and she was running a fever.

"Sophie, would you run an errand for me?" Mother asked, glancing nervously at the black sky. "Sister Grant said I might have some of her homemade ointment for Lucy, and I fear we need it. The poor little thing is suffering so. If you hurry fast you can make it before the storm breaks."

Eliza Grant lived nearly a mile down the road. But Sophie didn't mind. She liked walking, and she welcomed an excuse to go outdoors today.

"I'll be careful. And I'll hurry," she promised.

The wind was rising, whispering through the tall grasses at Sophie's feet. The high green branches of the trees swayed, as if to a lullaby. And, except for the sweet wind, the whole earth seemed still. Still and waiting, waiting for the cool rain the clouds would bring.

Sister Grant was both kind and efficient. She  gave Sophie a glass of buttermilk to drink while she scooped the ointment out of a large jar into a small earthenware pot. "I've got plenty and to spare," she assured Sophie. "With six little ones of my own, I always keep a supply made up and on hand. And here are some fresh-baked cookies for you and your brother."

She handed Sophie one to eat hot while she wrapped a generous number in cheesecloth. Then, placing the bundles in Sophie's arms, she gently pushed her toward the door.

"You be quick, now, my girl. I don't want you to get a soaking, and your mother to worry."

Sophie scurried out under the canopy of clouds that was settling lower and lower. It had grown as dark as a winter twilight. She shivered a little as the cool air prickled along her skin. The faster she walked the closer the sky churned above her. The wind tore at her coat with cold fingers. The trees shuddered and groaned beneath the force of the now bold and blustery wind. As Sophie struggled on, it seemed she was alone in the world, and the fierce storm might entirely swallow her up.

When the rain came, it came all at once. A wet drop on her nose, another on her cheek. Then the whole sky was water. Sophie tucked the bundles under the flap of her coat and tried to shield her face with her other hand. But it was no use. How much farther did she have? Probably less than a quarter of a mile. The lashing rain blinded her sight, but the road was well marked before her, and she knew the way.

She saw the overturned cart as soon as she rounded the curve. But she nearly stumbled against the body that lay huddled beside the up-turned wheel. She stopped, horrified, her heart pounding in her chest. What in the world should she do? This poor man had obviously met with an accident. But what could she do to help?

She bent closer. The man on the ground tried to move, but then moaned, and muttered something under his breath.

Sophie drew back with a gasp. She would recognize that bristly face anywhere! This was the mean old farmer who had scolded her and Ellen so cruelly—who had threatened both them and the boys. She stood trembling. Had he seen her? Would he remember? Couldn't she just hurry on—around the small wreck—and pretend she had never seen it? No one would know. And it would certainly serve him right, the old cross-patch!

Sophie stepped through the mud of the road-side gingerly. The wind tugged at her skirts and her strands of wet hair. She closed her eyes, and suddenly she saw the Prophet's face—his blue eyes gentle and smiling. And the words he had

spoken came back to her clearly: *Let love, not fear, dictate your actions.* The words startled Sophie. She paused and looked back over her shoulder. The man still lay there, crumpled and wet in the roadway. *Love him?* Then the Prophet's words came again: *Don't be stingy with your love, Sophie. Your father isn't.*

Sophie shuddered. She knew what she must do. The words echoed inside her head: *Your father isn't . . . Your father isn't . . .* She could see her father's black eyes smiling encouragement to her. She stumbled back to the spot where the old man lay. Without letting herself stop to think, she put her hand on his arm and began to shake him gently.

"I've come to help you!" she cried into the bluster of the wind. "Can you stand? I don't live very far from here. If you lean on me, can you manage to walk?"

The man's eyes opened. They were mere slits in his gray face. He grunted and nodded his head very slowly. Then his arm moved. His big gnarly hand reached up to her. Sophie leaned over and grasped it tightly with both of her own.

The quarter mile seemed endless. Sophie's arms ached, her back ached, even her head ached when she stumbled at last into her own yard, call-

ing out for Mother, who must have
been watching for her. In no time
at all both Sophie and the bristly
old man were safe in Mother's
warm kitchen, wiped dry with
towels, drinking hot broth
and eating the crushed remains of the cookies Sophie had

brought back from Sister Grant's. The old man's
eyes were watery with fatigue and gratitude. The
hardness had all gone out of them—though his
voice was still gruff and gravelly as he asked
Mother question after question. Sophie slipped
away after a few minutes to see to the baby and
rub the soothing ointment over her sores. The
rain didn't stop. Mother invited the old man to
have supper with them. She gave him dry clothes
to wear—clothes that were Father's! What had
gotten into her? She was talking with the stranger
as though she knew him well, as though they
were friends, as though—but then, Mother didn't
know about the old man and what he had done!
Would she be angry—would she stop being so
kind if Sophie told her how rough and mean he
had been?

Sophie ate quietly. Mother and the man kept
talking. He was telling her about his own life—
how he had married the girl he had loved all

through his childhood when they both were eighteen. She had borne him three children and then died of a fever. His voice grew as gray as his face when he talked of it. "She died when I was away, you see. She had been in bed for so many weeks and she longed for the sight of flowers— the fresh smell of them. I went out to the woods that stretched behind our homestead and gathered a right pretty bunch. I brought them inside and laid 'em down by her cheek. 'Here you are, dear heart,' I said. 'They smell as sweet as heaven, and they're nearly as pretty as you.'"

The man seemed to choke. His voice was thin and faint. Sophie had to lean forward to catch his last words. "She never saw them. She had gone without me—and I not there beside her to say good-bye."

Sophie thought of Mother and Father, the way they looked long and soft into each other's eyes. Could it have been like that with this old man and the pretty young wife who had left him?

Sophie had never seen Mother more gentle. The rain ceased, the harsh wind dropped, but their guest still stayed. At last Mother sent Oscar over to ask Brother Hobson to come with his wagon and team. Mother walked out with Isaac Porter—which was the old man's proper name— and fussed over him, tucking a blanket around his legs where he sat on the wagon seat. Sophie had never seen the like of it. What had come over Mother?

When Mr. Porter asked for Sophie, and Mother made her come out to the wagon, fear made her heart pound and her muscles go stiff.

"I mean to apologize to you," he said gruffly, "before I go. I never did cotton much to children, but you did a real decent thing, helping me back there on the road."

Sophie's mouth felt dry. She didn't know what to reply to him. But he didn't seem to expect her to say anything. He had already turned his head away from her. Brother Hobson clucked to the horses, and the wagon pulled out into the muddy, pocked road.

Mother stood watching after them, her arm around Sophie.

"I don't like him," Sophie said under her breath. "One day we ran into him on the road and scattered his pigs by accident, and he hit me with his stick and shouted terrible things. I should have told you then, but I was afraid you'd stop us from going to play by the river."

Mother stroked Sophie's hair gently. "But you helped him. You returned good for evil, Sophie. And you found, instead of an enemy, a tired and friendless old man."

Mother bent low and brushed her soft lips against Sophie's cheek. "Father will be so proud of you, Sophie."

Sophie knew Mother's words were true. A warm feeling spread all through her. Someone else would be proud of her actions, as well—the tall prophet with the kind, piercing eyes who had told her to let love guide her actions, and trust to the Lord for the rest.

Chapter
Five

FAITH
REWARDED

July melted into August. Bees swarmed in the clover, and mosquitoes festered the low, brown banks of the river. At home the hard green tomatoes grew heavy and ripe on the vines. Willow, the gray kitten Mother had given to Sophie, caught her first mouse. And Lucy Anne, her hair like the golden fluff of newborn chickens, took her first tottering steps.

"She'll be walking by the time Davey comes," Mother promised. "Now that she's got the hang of it, we won't be able to stop her." She was pleased. A pink blush glowed on her cheeks at the thought of it. She had received word that the Prophet had disbanded Zion's Camp once they reached Clay County, Missouri. The men were making their way home in smaller groups the best way they could. How long would it take? Was Father safe? Sophie got an achy feeling in her stomach every time she thought about him.

One fair morning Mother sent Sophie to Sister Shumway's store with a basket of tomatoes, beans, and peppers to sell, or to trade for needles and threads and spices. It was early; the sun had not yet burned the dew from the grasses and the leaves, low and heavy, that brushed with a cool swish-swish against Sophie's arm. The basket was heavy, and she wished she had Ellen's wagon to carry it in. She stopped often to rest, and to listen to the sweet, clear trill of the larks calling to one another. When she reached  the center of town it was already crowded with people. She moved with her head down, as quickly as she could, carrying her heavy, awkward burden.

"That's right. There's been trouble in Missouri. Armed men rode into the camp, I heard tell." The man's voice rose above the general confusion, and Sophie froze. Trouble in Zion's Camp!

"That isn't the half of it," his companion

added. "Ben Anderson got back day before yes-
terday. He said the cholera struck the men—"

That dread word *cholera* turned Sophie's
blood cold. Cholera attacked the stomach and in-
testines and could kill its victim in less than a day.
Sophie was so stunned that she didn't see the
boys coming up behind her. She didn't hear their
whoop of delight until it was too late—until they
had snatched the heavy basket from the board-
walk where she had rested it. Instinctively she
lunged, taking a few steps forward. But the boys
made faces and laughed out loud at her.

"Thanks for the good Mormon vegetables,
missy. That was mighty kind of you!"

Their laughter cut through her like a cold
wind. She held her arms out beseechingly. One of
the boys aimed and threw a large, soft tomato. It
hit beneath her collarbone with a sickening plop
and exploded in a red rain of juice and seeds all
across the front of her dress, staining her cheeks
and stinging her eyes. Through a mist of tears
Sophie saw the grin on the boy's crude features
suddenly contort. She saw him rise, as though
someone was lifting him, dangling him; she heard
him cry out like a—like a stuck pig! She wiped
her eyes clean with the hem of her apron and
watched, amazed, as Isaac Porter—his small eyes
narrow and angry—marched behind the startled

boy with his hand clamped hard on his neck. He shoved the unhappy culprit forward.

"I b'lieve you owe this young lady an apology," he growled. The boy's friends hung back, their eyes wide and frightened.

The boy muttered something. But it wasn't good enough for Isaac Porter. He tightened his hold and the boy squirmed. "We can't hear you, lad!" the old man snarled.

"I beg your pardon, miss. I'm sorry about the tomato and—and about your dress."

Isaac glared menacingly at the others, who shrank from his gaze. "Any of you fellows get it into your head in the future to bother this gal here—or any of her kin or her friends, for that matter—you'll find yourselves answering to me." He brought his long stick down with a whack against the boy's leg. "Do I make myself clear?"

There was no argument. Isaac made the culprits bring the basket forward, with the remains of Sophie's produce. When at last he released them with a curt nod, they scattered like mice from a woodpile when the cat is let loose.

He took a big faded handkerchief from his back pocket and wiped Sophie's face, then her stained dress front. He was a bit awkward, but there was a tenderness in his eyes she had never seen there before.

"You come with me," he said. "We'll get top dollar for those vegetables, my dear." He took her by the hand, cradling her basket in his other arm, his walking stick hanging from the crook of his elbow. Sophie was too startled and amazed to do anything but follow along with him.

"That young scoundrel who stole your goods," he explained as they walked. "Well, you see, his folks run a store just down the street a ways. I b'lieve his mother may be persuaded to deal generously with you."

When Sophie told Mother what had happened in town her eyes filled with a quiet pleasure. "I guess Mr. Porter isn't as old and tired as I thought he was," she smiled.

"*I* could have told you that," Sophie said.

But Sophie's other news—about cholera in Zion's Camp—brought that colorless, haunted expression to Mother's eyes. During the next few days it seemed as if a cloud hung over them, day and night. Sophie had never prayed so hard for anything in all her young life as she did for Father's safety. Mother's face began to look thin and drawn again. She even found it hard to laugh at Lucy Anne's antics.

One night, in the pale summer twilight, Sophie knelt at her bedside. She began to pray—the same old prayer that God would protect her dear father and bring him home to them safe and sound. Then a voice echoed in her head, speaking words she knew, but had somehow forgotten: *Do not fear, little one. As your father promised you, the Lord will take care of his own.*

It was fear that had made her forget. A quiet peace settled upon her. God would take care of her father—he would take care of them—as he always had.

Oscar, playing with Willow in the yard, was the first to spy him. He ran and threw himself into his father's arms and rode triumphantly atop his broad shoulders the rest of the way to the house. Mother, kneading bread in the kitchen, dropped her heavy rolling pin and ran to embrace him, not even dusting the flour off her apron and hands.

Sophie drank in the sight of him. He was thin, and that made him look taller. His faded clothes hung loose on his frame. His skin was toughened and bronzed by the sun. But his black eyes, when they found hers, sparkled with the same light, the same pleasure that had always been there.

"And how is my little nut-brown maiden?"

he asked. Then he opened his arms, and she ran
to him.

"There were hard times," Father said. His
voice was low. Sophie could feel the sadness in it.
"There was sickness and suffering in plenty, even
death for some." Shadows from the fire played
across his sensitive face. "But when we were
obedient and united, the Lord blessed us."

"What do you mean?" Mother asked.

"Well, there was the time when five armed
men rode into our camp threatening that we
would not live until morning. Though there was
not a cloud in the sky, a storm blew up suddenly,
driving the mobbers to huddle for protection in
an empty schoolhouse, and making it impossible
for them to come up against us. And just a few
days before that, a group of mobbers who were
heading by boat to Independence to raise an
army were sunk in the Missouri and seven were
drowned."

"The Lord protected you, didn't he?" Oscar
asked.

"Yes, my lad, he did. One of the mobbers
even remarked how strange it was that they could
do nothing against the Mormons but what something must come to hinder them."

"Were you sick, Father?" Sophie asked.

"Sick nigh unto death, it seemed to me," he replied. Then, seeing the concern in Mother's face, he smiled. "God was with us, my dear. As the Prophet himself said, 'We know that angels were our companions, for we saw them.'"

He bent over and lifted Lucy Anne into his arms and bounced her lovingly on his knee.

Angels. Sophie gazed at Father's calm, gentle face. Had he looked upon angels?

Father lifted his face and smiled at each of them in turn. "I don't regret going, not for one minute," he said firmly. "We were under the sweet influence of the Prophet, we witnessed miracles—and we learned how to love." His beautiful eyes smiled deeply into Sophie's. "Do you understand what that means, my nut-brown maiden?"

Sophie smiled back. Her heart was light; her whole body felt washed with light and happiness. "I understand, Father," she replied. And she did.

HIGHLIGHTS FROM HISTORY

Kirtland, Ohio
1831–1838

Kirtland, Ohio, was the first official gathering place of the restored Church of Jesus Christ (which would be designated by divine revelation in 1838 as The Church of Jesus Christ of Latter-day Saints). When Joseph Smith knelt and prayed in the grove outside his house near Palmyra, New York, he was only a lad of fourteen. But he had been taught by good parents the value of prayer. When God the Father and his Son, Jesus Christ, appeared to the boy and instructed him, he believed them. So

First edition of the Book of Mormon

did his parents, Joseph Smith Sr. and Lucy Mack Smith. They supported their son when the angel Moroni appeared to him and instructed him to uncover and then translate an ancient record written on gold plates which told the history of Moroni's own people, the early inhabitants of the American continent. Despite hardship and opposition from enemies, and even from friends and neighbors, Joseph completed his work. The translated record, known as the Book of Mormon, was published in March 1830.

Less than two weeks later, on 6 April 1830, the Church, established by revelation, was officially organized. Even before this, Joseph and his followers had been seeking new converts. Now, with the Book of Mormon as a tool, many missionaries went forth to convert their neighbors to the doctrines which had burned with such fire in their own hearts. One of the places they established a branch of the Church was in Kirtland, Ohio.

At a conference, or special meeting of the whole Church, held 2 January 1831 at Fayette, New York, the Lord instructed his people to move to Ohio. Several hundred new Latter-day Saints left their homes and families to answer the call.

Northeastern Ohio, part of what was called the Western Reserve, was looked upon as a land of milk and honey. The village of Kirtland stood on the banks of the Chagrin River, and at the crossroads of two major pioneer highways. The population of the quiet village before 1830 was less than a thousand. By 1838 the Mormon population alone numbered over two thousand. Such large numbers of people pouring in made it almost impossible to find places to live. One historical source states: "Every available house, shop, hut, or barn was filled to its utmost capacity. Even boxes were roughly extemporized and used for shelter until something more permanent could be secured." (*History of Geauga and Lake Counties,* quoted in *Encyclopedia of Mormonism,* ed. Daniel H. Ludlow, 5 vols. [New York: Macmillan, 1992], 2:795.) Most of the Saints arriving in Kirtland were in poor or modest conditions, despite the fact that many of them had previously enjoyed

Kirtland, Ohio

standards of financial success. John Tanner sold several flourishing businesses and properties, using part of the money to gather to Kirtland but donating the remainder of the proceeds to the Church. Brigham Young, a seasoned and successful businessman, had virtually nothing when he arrived in Kirtland, having left all behind in order to answer the Prophet's call.

In addition to these challenges there was persecution and violence from non-Mormon neighbors who resented the Latter-day Saints and were determined to thwart and hamper their progress. In March of 1832 Joseph Smith and Sidney Rigdon were tarred and feathered by a mob. As late as the winter of 1835 teenage boys, as well as men, were taking their turns sleeping in the Prophet's house as bodyguards. Benjamin F. Johnson remembered how, as a boy in Kirtland, he helped prepare arms for the protection of the Saints. For a time the lower part of his mother's house was fixed up as a gunsmith shop. (See *My Life's Review* [Mesa, Ariz.: 21st Century Printing, 1992], p. 24.) During the more troubled times men slept with their weapons tucked close beside them.

The family was of prime importance in the Mormon culture. Despite these difficulties, young men would be found working beside their fathers in the fields, chopping firewood and caring for animals, while the girls learned from their mothers how to cook over the primitive stoves, how to sew and mend, clean house, launder clothes, make soap and candles and other homemade implements such as household utensils and brooms. During the cold, dark winter months men spent much time at home with their families. Schools were held during these months as well. And Church meetings, singing schools, and prayer circles often took place at "early candlelight" when the people were free to gather together.

Not until 1836 was there a noticeable relief in conditions. Yet the Saints remained cheerful, busy, and productive, improving every opportunity that came their way and giving liberally of their time and means to build up the kingdom. Construction on the Kirtland Temple was begun in 1833. Six LDS mercantile firms were founded, as well as brickyards, forges, tanneries, shoe stores, lumber mills, and blacksmith shops. The Church itself operated a bank and a printing office. Men were outfitted as missionaries and sent off to the eastern states and Canada while their families managed without them.

After mobs destroyed the Church's press in Missouri, publication of *The Evening and the Morning Star* was resumed in Kirtland for a time, followed by the publication of the *Messenger and Advocate*. In 1833 the School of the Prophets was begun, and here priesthood holders had the opportunity for spiritual and intellectual training, studying a variety of subjects from the Lectures on Faith to history and Latin grammar. In the summer of 1834 over two hundred men (along with a small number of women and children), under direction of the Prophet, formed Zion's Camp and marched a thousand miles to Missouri to aid their fellow Saints.

And, through it all, work on the temple continued. On 27 March 1836, after three years of devotion and sacrifice, the temple was dedicated, and from late January to May 1836 the "Pentecost"—the outpouring of the Spirit—which Joseph Smith had promised was realized. Hundreds spoke in tongues, prophesied, or saw visions. Many, including children, saw angels or heard heavenly singing. The Savior appeared in five different meetings, and several people received visions.

There followed a blessed period of peace and harmony for the weary and faithful Saints. But persecution reared its head again, and the troubles in Kirtland became severe with the failure of the Kirtland Safety Society Anti-Banking Company.

Such bitter feelings prevailed that many members apostatized and actually sought the Prophet's life. As the weak fell by the wayside, the strong proved their loyalty and integrity and were blessed by God.

During these seven brief years the Mormons built not only a city but a way of life as well. Joseph Smith received and recorded dozens of new revelations.

Kirtland Temple pulpits

He made a translation of the Bible and of the Egyptian papyri which had come into his hands. The gospel was taken to hundreds of earnest, seeking people who willingly threw in their lot with the Saints. Men and women were prepared for the callings and challenges of the future, and a temple was built to the Most High God. Incredible accomplishments against almost insurmountable odds. But now it was time to move on. In January 1838, Joseph left Kirtland.

In the next seven months, over sixteen hundred Saints fled the city and traveled to western Missouri, where the majority gathered in Far West.

Though the fruits of their labors, including the stately and sacred temple, were left behind, most of the Latter-day Saints felt that their Kirtland experience was a valuable education in the things of the Spirit. In Joseph Smith's history, an entry describing a conference held in Kirtland in the summer of 1831 exemplifies the Saints' feelings about this period: "It was clearly evident that the Lord gave us power in proportion to the work to be done, and strength according to the race set before us, and grace and help as our needs required" (*History of the Church* 1:176). They were becoming the Lord's people—united, and confident in his power and his unfailing love.

About the Author

Susan Evans McCloud is the author of over twenty-five books. Those for children include *A. A. Seagull, I'm Going to Be Baptized, Black Stars over Mexico,* and *Jennie.* Mrs. McCloud has also written newspaper feature articles, scripts for filmstrips, screenplays, and lyrics—including two hymns for the 1985 Church hymnal. She is a part-time teacher of English and creative writing, and is a tour guide at Brigham Young's Beehive House. She and her husband, James, are the parents of six children, and the grandparents of three. Mrs. McCloud loves history, poetry, travel, flowers, Scottish music, and "tea" parties.

About the Artist

In addition to the pictures found in this book, Jessica Mormann Chopelas has drawn those found in two other books about Sophie—*Something Lost, Something Gained* and *The Angels Sing*—and has done the artwork for a book about baptism called *What Is White?* Mrs. Chopelas lives in Massachusetts with her husband, Karl, and their two children, Alexander and Julia. She enjoys the timeless crafts of bookbinding by hand, cultivating herbs, and processing sheep's wool. With Alex and Julia, Mrs. Chopelas loves to walk on the beach, read books, and visit farms.